EVERY SINGLE MOMENT

Every Single Moment

100 Powerful Prayers to Savor the Present & Prepare for the Future

stephanie may wilson

Every Single Moment
100 Powerful Prayers to Savor the Present and Prepare for the Future
By Stephanie May Wilson

RELIGION / Christian Life / Prayer

ISBN: 978-1-94429-856-2

Design by Luum Studio
HelloLuum.com

Printed in the United States of America

Table of Contents

Every Single Moment Matters

Dear Friend,

I started my very first journal in sixth grade. I had a new boyfriend named Erik, and I was entirely unsure how I felt about him (I mean, you remember sixth grade, right?). I purchased a small black journal with matte black pages, and in silver gel pen, I began pouring out everything I was thinking and feeling.

That journal started something very real and incredibly important in my life, and I've been journaling ever since—recording, day-by-day, the first, slightly sloppy draft of the story of my life.

I became a Christian at the end of college. That's when someone told me you could journal and pray at the same time; that writing your prayers to God was not only a way to keep your mind from wandering, but also a great way to keep a record of God's faithfulness in your life. It made perfect sense to me, and it fit how I already processed thoughts and emotions. Needless to say, I jumped on that train immediately. Fast forward nearly a decade and I have boxes and boxes of prayer journals. They're my most prized possession.

One of my favorite prayer journals is the one I kept in the season just before I met my husband, Carl. I was ready to meet my person, and it was painful watching so many of my friends meet their husbands first. It was a lonely season for me in a lot of ways, but it was also a rich, transformative, and wildly fun time in my life as well—and to be honest, I'm not sure if I would have noticed that without this habit of prayer journaling.

I was praying about a lot of things in those days—pouring out pages and pages of hopes, dreams, and fears. I was praying that God would help me become the woman He created me to be, and that He would use me to do big and beautiful things in the world. I was praying about my identity and my friendships, both of which felt a bit rocky in those days, and I wanted to see growth and change. I wanted to savor these days and to make the most of every single moment of this season of my life. In the midst of all of that, I was also praying for my future husband and for the life we'd build together.

Every single one of those prayers made a difference in my life back then and in my marriage today. Through them, God helped me heal from the past, live in the present, and prepare for the future in the most beautiful way.

Prayer journaling plays a central role in my life and I recommend it to everyone I meet—especially people navigating singleness, dating, and all the feelings this season brings with it.

A prayer journal invites you to peek into your heart, gather up what you find, and sort through it with God's help. As you open up these tender parts of yourself to God, He steps into them and changes you, redeems you, heals you, and transforms you in ways you might not even be able to imagine.

Prayer journals are also a great way to document your story as it's happening. Our lives go by quickly, and if you're anything like me, you can't even remember what you ate for dinner last week, let alone details that happened months or even years ago. I love having a record of what I was doing just weeks before I met my husband. I love re-reading my thoughts from the moments just before our first date. I love reading the prayers I was praying for our future marriage and seeing all the ways they've been answered.

Our journals are the first draft of our life story—our love story. They're a gift to our future selves, a beautiful keepsake documenting God's presence and faithfulness in our lives. That's what I pray this journal becomes for you.

I'm also praying that this prayer journal brings you peace.

The thing most people gloss over is the fact that prayer is hard. It's like folding a fitted sheet— we're never sure if we're doing it right. Prayer for your future person is even harder. There may be times when you don't pray into your future because you're not sure if it matters. I'm here to tell you that it does matter! After all, deciding who to marry will impact your life more than any other decision. You definitely want God to be a part of it. But sometimes, the opposite is true, and you might find yourself only praying about your future husband, idolizing both him and marriage. Prayer becomes a way to feel like you're living in a future that you haven't reached quite yet. When your focus is solely on the future, you risk missing out on the present, and it is actually living and praying in the present that will prepare you for that glowing future you dream of.

I created this prayer journal to help with the journey. It's a guide to help you make the most of every single moment by savoring the present, which is the very best way to prepare for your future life, your future marriage, and your future family. Best of all, this is a keepsake—a record of your story and the loving God who showed up in the midst of it. So, let's begin. Are you ready?

Pray that God would help you as you begin this prayer journey. Ask Him to help you be brave and bold and intentional with the next one hundred days. Ask Him to help you do the things you know you need to do to become the woman you want to be. Ask Him to meet you in the midst of this adventure, to answer your prayers, and to transform both you and your life along the way.

Know that I'll be praying for you the whole way through.

All my love,

Stephanie

DAY 1

"God, please be close."

It's a simple prayer, but it's one of my favorites, and I pray it all the time. Don't you love that your prayers can be just that simple? As you begin this new chapter with God, spend some time inviting Him to be close to you. You can pray the prayer I just mentioned and leave it at that, or you can add to the prayer if you have more to say. (You can also do what I do and pray those words over and over again—for me, sometimes it just helps.)

___

DAY 2

When I was single, I rarely talked about how I felt about it. I didn't want people to know I was struggling. I didn't even want to admit it to myself. At times, being single was hard enough in private. But if people knew that I didn't necessarily want to be single, that felt like public failure. The thing I learned though, is that my struggles didn't disappear because I was hiding them—they actually tended to get worse. Conversely, when I was able to shine a light on the hurting places within my heart, I started to heal and grow. Today, pray and ask God to help you be honest and open as you pray over these next three months.

_____

_____

_____

_____

_____

_____

_____

_____

_____

_____

DAY 3

Soon you're going to be talking, dreaming, and praying about your future relationships. But before you do that, let's spend some time talking about the past. What does your story look like? Have you dated a lot, a little bit, or not at all? Maybe you've been engaged before or maybe you've never been kissed. Today, spend some time telling God about your relationship history. (And if it feels like you don't have a past, go ahead and tell him that too!)

I know this conversation can be painful or feel awkward, but remember that honesty creates space for intimacy. The more you can share with God, the closer you'll start to feel to Him and the more you'll get to see Him show up in your life.

DAY 4

Are there any ways in which you feel like God has let you down? You were praying for this one thing, and it seems like He didn't come through. You were so hoping for this specific outcome, but it never came to be. Take a few minutes today to tell God about any disappointments you're carrying. You won't surprise Him or offend Him. He knows your innermost thoughts, and He loves you no matter what. Honest conversations are healing, and they are the first step towards intimacy. Take a deep breath and draw close to Him today.

_____

_____

_____

_____

_____

_____

_____

_____

_____

_____

_____

_____

DAY 5

Now that we've talked about the past, let's take a look at the present. How are you feeling about your current relationship status—your love life as it is today? Are you feeling lonely or impatient or frustrated? Are you hurting or anxious? Maybe you're feeling content right now. Whatever you're feeling is totally fine (and totally normal!). Practice honesty with God as you tell Him about this today. He's in this with you. You don't have to walk through this alone!

DATE:

DAY 6

How are you doing today? Spend a few minutes being quiet, checking in with yourself, and then share your findings with God. If you find an area where you could use some encouragement or strength, go ahead and ask for it! You serve a big and wonderful God who hears and answers your prayers.

DAY 7

Imagine that it's four years from now, and while your story hasn't unfolded exactly the way you planned it (they never do!), it's even better. Do you have that picture in your mind's eye? Write your current self a note with some advice and encouragement from that place. Four years from now, what will you wish you had done in this season of your life? Take a few minutes to give your current self the advice you think your older self would want you to have.

_____

_____

_____

_____

_____

_____

_____

_____

_____

_____

_____

_____

_____

_____

_____

DAY 8

Isaiah 41:13 says, "For I am the Lord your God who takes hold of your right hand and says to you, Do not fear; I will help you" (NIV). Spend a moment reflecting with God on what this promise means for your life today.

DAY 9

Zoom out past your day-to-day for a minute and consider your life as a whole. Overall, what is going well? Are there any parts of your life that aren't going so well? Are there any areas where you feel a bit lifeless? Share your discoveries with God and ask Him to breathe new life into any places that need it.

DAY 10

Imagine the day you meet your future husband. Close your eyes if you like. Picture the scene. Where are you? What are you doing? What is your first interaction like? Once you have a few of those details sketched out in your mind, move your attention to yourself. Who are you on the day you meet your husband? What qualities and characteristics are true about you? What does your life look like?

Make a list of a few things you want to be true about yourself on that life-changing day, and then spend a few minutes praying over them with God. Ask Him to help you take steps toward the version of yourself that you hope to be.

A Life of Delight

Dear Friend,

For as long as I can remember I've been the girl who says no.

"Do you want to play?"
"No thanks, I'll just watch!"

"Do you want to try this new thing?"
"Go ahead without me."

I've been that girl forever, and it's all because of fear.

It was the fear of looking silly by going beyond my comfort zone. It was the fear of embarrassing myself; of being bad at something. It was the fear of being rejected. Sometimes I think I was mostly just afraid of being afraid!

But a few years before I met my husband, I started realizing just how much I'd missed out on by letting fear decide what I do. By keeping myself only where I was comfortable, I'd missed out on so many wonderful adventures and experiences. So I decided to do something about it. I decided to start saying yes.

Saying yes isn't easy, but it really does change everything. Those yeses took me on some incredible adventures, and my life became so much more fun because of it. The same invitation is there for you. An enthusiastic "Yes!" will open doors, broaden your horizons, and allow you to fully taste and see just how good God can be.

God transformed me as I practiced saying "yes!" to His invitations—from traveling to new countries to the emotional work of growing and changing. By trying new things, I developed a dependence on God and a deep sense of self. I'm kinder, wiser, braver, and more loving because of the people I met and the experiences I had along the way. And actually, it was because I stepped out of my comfort zone and said yes to these opportunities that I was in the right place at the right time to meet my sweet husband!

It's amazing to look at myself and realize I'm no longer the person I used to be. I'm not held back by fear anymore, and you don't have to be either.

This next section of prayer is an invitation to live your single life to the fullest, and I'm so excited for you to journey through it! As you prepare to dive in, start by having an honest conversation with God. Are there areas of life where you're opting out, saying no, or letting fear hold you back? Share anything that comes to mind and ask Him for both the chances and the courage to start saying yes.

I'm praying for big bravery and a sense of excitement for what could come next!

Love,

Stephanie

DAY 11

Pray a bold prayer today: Ask God to help you make this season of your life the most transformative, joyful, rich, game-changing season possible. In fact, ask Him to help you make this season of life better and more wonderful than anything you can imagine!

EVERY SINGLE MOMENT

DAY 12

Poet Mary Oliver says, "Tell me, what is it you plan to do with your one wild and precious life?" Reflect on these words with God, and then ask Him for two things:

First, ask Him for opportunities to step out of your comfort zone, because after all, the best parts of life begin at the ends of our comfort zones!

Second, ask Him for the courage to say yes to those opportunities when they come.

_____

_____

_____

_____

_____

_____

_____

_____

_____

_____

_____

_____

DAY 13

Philippians 4:4–5 says, "Rejoice in the Lord always. I will say it again: Rejoice! Let your gentleness be evident to all. The Lord is near" (NIV).

It's easy to rejoice when you have exactly what you want, but that's not what this verse says. Paul doesn't say, "Rejoice in the Lord when everything is going your way." He says, "Rejoice in the Lord always."

What would it look like for you to really rejoice in this season of your life?

_____

_____

_____

_____

_____

_____

_____

_____

_____

_____

_____

_____

_____

DAY 14

Take a few minutes to write down three great things about being single. Think about opportunities that are available to you today that may not be available to you in future seasons. Then talk to God about some ways you can start to take advantage of these unique gifts!

DAY 15

Are you good at having fun? That's a pretty crazy question, isn't it? I started thinking about this last summer, and I've been thinking about it ever since.

As women, we are raised to be responsible adults who work hard to be good stewards of what we've been given. We're expected to manage our time, know how to budget, and excel at our jobs, not to mention be involved in our communities, families, and schools—the list goes on and on!

These things are all important, but life becomes so flat when we treat it as a list to check off instead of something to be savored. So again, I want to ask the question, are we good at having fun? Do we know how to enjoy our lives?

Have you ever asked yourself those questions?

That's my invitation for you today. Ask yourself, "Am I good at having fun?" and share your answer with God. Then, ask God to help you get better. Ask Him to help you get better at enjoying your life and being present for it. Ask God to help you get better at having fun!

DAY 16

God created each one of us on purpose and for a purpose. What's one gift you know God has given you? Maybe you're a fantastic teacher. Maybe you're really kind or a great listener. Maybe you have a passion for fighting the injustices of this world or a gift for making really great food. God put those things in you because He wants you to use them. He wants you to use them to love His people and to make His world a better, more beautiful place. What's one thing you know God has placed in you that He wants you to share with the world? Thank Him for that, and then spend a few minutes brainstorming one small way that you could share that gift this week.

DAY 17

How is work going for you these days? Spend a few minutes praying about your current work situation, and then ask God for any wisdom or direction you might need. Is there a promotion you've been dreaming about or a change you'd love to make but aren't sure if you can (or should)? Our jobs take up an enormous amount of space in our minds and our hearts and our days, yet all too often, we forget that we can pray about them. Spend some time today asking God for the things you need from Him to flourish at work.

DAY 18

What are your hobbies these days? As we get older and dive into our careers, we often stop having extracurricular activities. We used to love to paint, to dance, to sing, to play sports, but somewhere along the line we just... stopped. This doesn't have to be the case! We can still make time to pursue the things we love to do. And as a bonus, getting more involved with hobbies is a great way to meet new friends (and maybe even a great guy!). Spend some time telling God about things you used to love to do or about things you've always wanted to learn to do. When you're done, pull out your phone and do a quick online search for a class you could take or a club you could join. You'll be amazed at the opportunities you find!

DAY 19

Is there a dream that you've been putting off because you're afraid it'll take you away from meeting your person?

Today, spend a few minutes asking this simple (but important!) question: If you knew that God had the husband thing totally handled, what's a dream you'd want to pursue?

DAY 20

What are three things that are bringing you joy this week? Share them with God and then thank Him for them! These three things can be as big as your love for your family and as small as finally finding that perfect shade of nail polish—don't feel like there's any wrong answer here!

DAY 21

Are you the kind of woman who knows how to rest? A woman who is comfortable in moments of quiet and who refills in the presence of God? Spend a few moments reflecting on what rest looks like in your life right now. Are you sprinting through life these days? Or are you taking time to savor the little moments that make life so sweet? And if you could use some help slowing down and savoring more, don't be afraid to ask for that!

A Life of Faith

Dear Friend,

It cannot be overstated: the very best thing that I did while I was single was to invest deeply in my relationship with God. It truly changed everything for me.

When God swooped into my life, He brought redemption, meaning, joy, and a fresh start. God has helped me make incredible friends, pursue my dreams, and feel beautiful and like I'm enough in my own skin. He brought me into an adventurous, purpose-filled life that has been more wild and more wonderful than anything I ever could have dreamt up on my own. And those adventures are the reason I was in the right place at the right time to meet my sweet husband. God is deeply woven into the fabric of our relationship, and because of that, our marriage has been richer and more wonderful than I could have ever imagined.

If you've made it this far in the prayer journal, I think it's safe to say you hope for a beautiful, godly marriage. I did too! But what I have come to understand is that a godly marriage isn't just two people who occasionally read a devotional together. A godly marriage is when two people who deeply love God decide to love Him together. And the great news is, you have half of that equation long before you have a clue who your husband will be!

Your personal relationship with God is the cornerstone for everything: today, tomorrow, and forever, amen. The best thing you can do for your life today and your marriage down the road is to deeply invest in your relationship with Jesus.

That's exactly what this next section is all about. As you work through it, my prayer for you is that you experience intimacy, grace, and affection from the Lord in brand new ways, and that the next several days begin a new chapter where you feel closer to Him than ever before.

Are you ready? Let's dive in!

Love,

Stephanie

DAY 22

What does your relationship with God look like today? Do you feel close to Him? Do you feel like you have a thriving spiritual life? What are some ways you'd like to grow in your relationship with God? What are some things you may want to be different a year from now?

After you think through this, spend a few minutes asking God for the growth you desire. You can ask God for help with every single part of your life, including your relationship with Him. Isn't that amazing?!

DAY 23

There's nothing you can do to make God love you more than He does right now, and there's nothing you can do to make God love you less than He does right this second. Because of Jesus, you're in good standing with God. He loves you, you have access to Him, and He wants a relationship with you—right this second, and forever. Take some time to journal about how it feels to hear that truth today.

DAY 24

The more time you spend with someone, the closer you feel to them. Think of a first date or the first time you hung out with a friend. Those first few interactions can definitely feel a bit awkward, but each time you connect with that person, you feel closer and more comfortable with them! This is true with God too.

Practice having an honest conversation with God today. Tell Him how you're doing, what's on your mind, what's going well in your life, and what might not be going so well. Approaching Him in a more conversational and intimate way will help you feel closer to Him, and you'll get to rest in the knowledge that you don't have to carry these things on your own.

DAY 25

What's causing you stress today? Take a moment to write whatever is stressing you out on a piece of paper and tuck it in your Bible or another safe place. There's no magic to this; it's just a physical representation of the fact that you're handing this over to God. He can take care of it. He has it covered. (Then, check out Matthew 6:25–34!)

DAY 26

Do you ever find yourself wrestling with guilt? I certainly do sometimes. It's so tempting to hide from God when you're feeling guilty about something, but have you noticed that hiding never actually makes it better? God promises that when His children confess their sins to Him, He will be faithful to forgive and to repair what has been broken. Will you be brave and believe that in your life today?

Talk to God about anything that's making you feel guilty; be honest about it, confess it, and invite Him into it. Ask Him to forgive you, and to show you a better way. He'll answer that prayer. You can trust Him.

DAY 27

Psalm 86:5 says, "You, Lord, are forgiving and good, abounding in love to all who call to you" (NIV). Today, make a list of other things you know to be true about God's character. This is one of the best things you can do to help your faith grow!

EVERY SINGLE MOMENT

DAY 28

It can be so easy to forget that God is a good Father when you're waiting or hoping for something, but that doesn't change the facts. God is a sovereign Father who gives good gifts to His children. Pausing to remember the stories of how He has been faithful in your life and in other people's lives is a powerful way to build your faith. Spend a few minutes thinking about where you've seen God show up for you (or one of your girlfriends) lately, and then thank God for His provision in both of your lives.

DAY 29

Did you know that you can ask God to use the pain in your life for good? It's often in the moments where your heart is broken open or when your plans come to a halt (or crumble completely), that you can see God move the most because that's when you can best experience His comfort, peace, and hope.

Take a few minutes to invite God into a place where you're hurting today. Ask Him to repair and redeem the thing that feels broken. Then, pray that He would use this bruised piece of your heart as a catalyst for something new and beautiful in your life.

DAY 30

What was going on in your life this time three years ago? How has God shown up in your life since then? How has He provided for you, changed things, and changed you? Spend some time reflecting on that today.

DAY 31

God's plan for your life is better than anything you could come up with on your own, and His timing is always right. Spend a few minutes processing that truth with God today and ask Him to help you really believe in His goodness—especially in moments when you're tempted to compare your life to someone else's.

DAY 32

Spend a few minutes soaking in Paul's prayer for the Ephesians. This is one of my favorite prayers to pray over people I love, and over myself. There's something so helpful about writing out God's word, so, in the space below, re-write Paul's prayer, substituting your name for all of the "you's." Make it personal! Practice reading these words out loud to yourself. It's a powerful prayer that I know God wants to answer in your life.

Here's Paul's prayer:

"I pray that out of His glorious riches He may strengthen you with power through His Spirit in your inner being, so that Christ may dwell in your hearts through faith. And I pray that you, being rooted and established in love, may have power, together with all the Lord's holy people, to grasp how wide and long and high and deep is the love of Christ, and to know this love that surpasses knowledge—that you may be filled to the measure of all the fullness of God."
– Ephesians 3:16–19 (NIV)

A Life of Friendship

Dear Friend,

When you're single, it can feel like your life is totally devoid of meaningful relationships, but that's not actually true! When my love life felt sorely lacking, there was another, equally important set of relationships that totally thrived: my friendships.

One of the absolute best parts of this season is all the time you can spend investing in your friendships. Honestly, I'm not sure I would have survived my single and dating life without my girlfriends by my side— it certainly wouldn't have been as much fun without them!

For every first date that went horribly wrong, there were dozens of girls' nights full of pizza and inside jokes and terrible movies we'd all seen twenty times. During this season, we lived together, we traveled together, and we navigated first jobs and big decisions together.

My girlfriends have been some of the most foundational and transformational relationships in my life. That has translated into marriage as well.

Just as we navigated singleness and dating together, now we are navigating marriage together. I'm such a better wife because I have them in my corner, and I love getting to cheer them on in their marriages too. I'm so glad we don't have to do any of this alone!

It may not always feel like it, but you actually have two really unique gifts during your season of singleness and dating: time and proximity for life-defining friendships. At some point in the future, you will be married, you and your girlfriends will be living with your husbands, and who knows what corners of the world everyone ends up in?!

Your friendships will still be amazing (and your trips to visit will be extra sweet!), but you won't ever have as much time for one another as you do right now. This is the perfect time to build a foundation for the kind of community you're going to want forever—and these friendships will make every season of life better, easier, and absolutely more fun. Today, I have the most wonderful best friends because I invested in them when we were single.

Maybe the idea of all these great friendships sounds more like a dream than a reality for you right now. Maybe you're looking around your life and feeling really lonely. Maybe you just moved to a new city or your friends just moved away (or got married or had a baby, which sometimes can feel like the same thing). Maybe you're feeling distant from the people who used to be your people, or maybe you feel like you've never quite found your people.

If you're in this place right now, please know that you're not alone. I know it seems like everyone already has their best friends, but I promise you that's not true. So many women are walking around feeling lonely and disconnected. You're not alone in feeling this way!

Just as important—it's never too late to start a new chapter in your friendship story! It's never too late to find your best friend, to find your people. It takes some time and intentionality, but you can do that! And the friendships you'll form as a result could change your life. I promise!

As you pray through your friendships in this section, I'm praying that this kicks off a journey towards more love and connection than you've ever dared to dream about. I'm praying that this will be the push you need to invest even more deeply in the women around you and that your friendships will grow like crazy.

I'm also praying that one day, when you look back on this season, you'll remember it as a time you felt deeply known and loved by women who grew into lifelong friends—one epic girls' night at a time.

Love,

Stephanie

DAY 33

Let's begin today with an update. Spend some time telling God what friendships look like for you right now. Does your community feel rich and full or maybe a little sparser than it used to? Do you have friends who are in the same season of life as you, or are most of your friends engaged, married, or even having babies right now? Are you in a season where you're wishing for more (or deeper) friendships? Spend some time telling God about your friendships today.

DAY 34

When it comes to the topic of friendship, what hesitations, fears, doubts, or even excuses do you find popping up in your head? Maybe you feel like you don't have the time to invest in friendships, or maybe you've tried to pursue friendships, but it feels like you've failed.

Spend a few minutes talking to God today about the things that hold you back from truly putting yourself out there and investing in friendships. Then, pray a bold prayer and ask Him for the help you need to break through those obstacles.

EVERY SINGLE MOMENT

DAY 35

Have you ever felt like giving up on the whole concept of friendship? Maybe you've been betrayed, left out, or gossiped about. The idea of making new friends could sound like opening yourself up to that hurt all over again.

Take a few minutes to talk through this with God today. Tell Him about any painful experiences that come to mind when you think about the idea of friendship in your life. Then, ask Him to come into those places where you're hurting.

We serve a God who brings life from death, beauty from ashes, and hope from despair. He's done that in my heart in the midst of some of my hardest, most painful friendship experiences, and I know He can do the very same thing for you. All you have to do is ask. Ask Him for healing and redemption for your friendships today.

DAY 36

Our lives are seriously impacted by the people we spend the most time with, so it's important that we consciously choose people who lift us up and help us grow into our best selves.

Spend a few minutes today reflecting on the people who surround you and the people you see most often. Do they bring out the best in you? Are they kind? Are they good friends?

These are hard questions to ask, because an honest answer could require you to make some tough choices. But God is faithful to provide for all of your relationships—and your friendships count big time!

Take some time to reflect on your friendships today and ask God for wisdom on how to move forward in them.

DAY 37

In order to be the best versions of ourselves, we need a web of support from different types of people. Think about the friends you have from different areas of your life. Do you have a friend or two who share your faith, and maybe someone else who totally gets your work life? Do you have wise people who you can go to for advice?

Spend some time thinking through this today and ask God to help you identify any areas where you could use a bit more support in your life!

_____

_____

_____

_____

_____

_____

_____

_____

_____

_____

_____

_____

DAY 38

If you could snap your fingers and have your friendships look a certain way this time next year, what would you hope to see? Spend a few minutes dreaming with God today.

DAY 39

It would be wonderful if you always experienced the exact same thing on the exact same day as your friends, but unfortunately that's rarely the case. Your friend gets into a relationship the same day you get out of one. You get a promotion on the same day she gets let go. While this can be super hard, it's not the end of those friendships. Not even close. Romans 12:15 says, "Rejoice with those who rejoice; mourn with those who mourn" (NIV). When you find yourself going through different (and even opposite!) things, you can practice that kind of love by building a bridge and joining each other on opposite shores for a while, rejoicing and mourning with each other so you don't have to do either alone.

Think through your friendships right now and consider where you might start building a bridge to meet a friend. How can you truly celebrate with a friend who just got engaged? How can you support your friend and her brand-new baby? And how can you communicate with your friends more clearly about what you need in this season?

DAY 40

Who are you especially grateful for right now? Do you have a friend at work who's made your days so much easier and more fun? A new friend who said just the right thing in the moment you needed to hear it, or an old friend who has been particularly awesome lately? Thank God for the gift of friendship in your life, and then send that person a quick text to let them know how much they mean to you.

DAY 41

We're so much more likely to achieve a goal when we have people keeping us accountable. Goals go from out of reach to totally possible when you have a community surrounding you and encouraging you to keep going! Write down a few goals you're working toward and ask God to help you connect with women who are pursuing similar things. Ask Him to help you find women who will cheer you on, encourage you to stay on track, pray for you, and laugh with you along the way (and women who you can support too!). The journey is so much more fun when you're on it together. Pray for some travel buddies today.

DAY 42

Speaking of travel buddies, are there any adventures you've been wanting to go on, things you've been wanting to try, or places you've been wanting to explore, but you feel like you can't because you don't have anyone to go with?

It's so frustrating to want to make the most of this season, but to feel limited in what you can do on your own. Spend a few minutes talking to God about any dreams you have or adventures you might want to go on. Pray that He'd open up doors for you to do those things, and that He'd help you connect with people who want to do them too.

DAY 43

Have you ever been hit square in the face with comparison? You're walking along through life, feeling good enough, strong enough, beautiful enough, and then it happens . . . WHAM! Comparison.

It happens for all kinds of reasons, and it can come on like food poisoning—sudden, strong, and totally debilitating. "Why her? Why not me? What's wrong with me? Why doesn't my life look like hers?"

Talk to God about a time when this has happened to you, or about a friend you consistently compare yourself to.

Ask Him to set you free, to heal that place in your heart, and to help you remember the truth: God loves you, He created you with a purpose, the way He created you is absolutely good enough, and there's more than enough goodness in the world to go around.

_____

_____

_____

_____

_____

_____

_____

DAY 44

Are there any areas of your life where you find yourself particularly prone to comparison? Take some time to reflect and recognize those trouble spots, and then ask God to heal them and to help you rejoice in the fact that He sees you, He knows you, He loves you, and He has a wonderful story written uniquely for you.

If you could see the story God is writing in your life, you'd never be jealous of anyone else's. I promise!

_____

_____

_____

_____

_____

_____

_____

_____

_____

_____

_____

_____

_____

_____

DAY 45

As you finish this time of praying for your friendships, I invite you to pray a brave, bold prayer. Spend a few minutes today asking God to bring amazing best friends into your life—the kind of friends you've always, always wanted. Ask Him for the courage, perseverance, and energy to play the part that's yours to play in bringing those friendships to life. Last but not least, spend a moment thinking of one small thing you can do today to either make a new friend or grow closer to one you already have. I dare you to take that one small step today.

A Life of Confidence

Dear Friend,

I was talking to a girlfriend a few years ago when she told me, "If I just had someone to love me, then I think I could finally love myself."

I nodded as she spoke—I've had that thought more than once, after all. But I've also learned from experience that you can be in a wonderful, loving relationship and still feel totally and incurably unlovable. I've learned that nobody can love us into loving ourselves, no matter how much we may want them to.

I had to learn this lesson the hard way.

More than once, I found myself dating a guy who truly loved me. He loved me, he treated me well, he thought I was great, and he told me so! But no matter how well he treated me, no matter how much he loved me, it never made me feel any better. It never actually helped me feel loved.

No matter what anybody else did and no matter how much

someone else loved me, nobody could love me enough to convince me I was worthy of it.

So, there we were, nice guys pouring love in and me, always hungry for more. It was painful for me, frustrating for them, and destined to fail. While it was never the official reason we broke up, it was always part of it.

After doing this dance several times, I eventually saw the pattern, and I knew I had to make a change.

I knew that God says I'm loved, that I'm perfectly and wonderfully made, and what I began to realize is that I didn't believe Him. But I desperately wanted to. I made it my mission to start learning about and stepping into my God-given identity. I wanted to start loving myself the way He loves me. I had a feeling that if I could do that, it would change my life. And it did.

As I began to embrace and embody my God-given identity, I started to live with so much more freedom, courage, joy, and confidence. I was learning to see myself the way God sees me—in other words, I was learning to love myself.

My life got so much better when I started loving myself. It changed how I felt in my skin every single day, and the changes rippled out from there. My dating life got so much better too. When I wasn't scrounging for affirmation, I found that it came so much more easily.

There was an intangible shift in me, and people took notice.

And it didn't stop there either. Working on my relationship with myself is one of the very best things I have ever done for my marriage. Because I'm secure in my identity in Christ, I'm not looking to Carl to love me enough for the both of us and I can actually receive and enjoy his love. And because I feel loved, because I feel good enough and worthy, I'm able to love Carl right back. My ability to love myself transformed our marriage before it even started.

Friend, we all struggle with broken identity in one way or another. For some of us, insecurity is positively crippling. For others, it's more like an annoying fly we can't seem to shake. Regardless of how insecurity shows up in your life, understanding (and believing!) what God says about you is a crucial step in your story.

God has so much to say about who you are and what you're worth, and when you begin to really believe Him, it changes everything. It has for me, and I know it will for you too.

When you're ready, go ahead and dive into the prayer prompt on the next page. Know that I'm praying with you.

Love,

Stephanie

DAY 46

Friend, let's start with a tough question: how do you feel about yourself? How do you treat yourself? Do you feel worthy of love, and even trickier, do you treat yourself like someone who is worthy of love? Spend some time reflecting on this with God, and then write a list of three things you love about yourself.

DAY 47

What are the most common things your inner critic says to you? Are there ways in which you can see your inner critic stealing joy from you or keeping you from doing the things you know God created you to do?

Think through those questions with God today. Share with Him anything that comes to mind, and then pray that He would adjust your thoughts about yourself to match His. Trust me, you want to see yourself the way He sees you.

DAY 48

Think through any insecurities you may be carrying and bring them to God today. Then, pray a big, bold prayer and ask Him to set you free.

_____

_____

_____

_____

_____

_____

_____

_____

_____

_____

_____

_____

_____

_____

_____

_____

DAY 49

Insecurity has the power to absolutely cripple your love life. It's hard to accept and reciprocate someone's love when you don't think you're worthy of it. And it's impossible to put yourself out there when you think no one will ever choose you.

Friend, when you look at your love life—past and present, and when you think about what the future may hold—can you see any ways in which insecurity may be holding you back? Do you think your love life could be better if you felt more confident and more worthy of love? Reflect on that with God today. Ask Him to fill you up with the truth of how loved and how worthy of love you truly are.

DAY 50

God loves you and has chosen you.
1 Thessalonians 1:4

You were created by God to do good, beautiful things.
Ephesians 2:10

You are a child of God.
John 1:12

God delights in you.
Zephaniah 3:17

You are beautiful. There is no flaw in you.
Song of Songs 4:7

Those are just some of the things God says to be true about you, and they're true even when it doesn't feel like it. Take a few minutes to read these truths out loud (personalize them so they're about you!), and then in the space below, ask God to help you fully believe them about yourself.

_____

_____

DAY 51

Love requires vulnerability and risk, and even when you're secure in your identity, it really hurts when those things don't result in the connection you're hoping for.

Here's a hard truth: while knowing your worth and being solid in your identity in Christ is the cornerstone of building a healthy relationship, it can't protect you from all pain—it's not supposed to. You can know who you are and how much you're worth, and still feel the pain of rejection when he doesn't text back.

Ask God to help you remember who you are, whose you are, and how truly loved you are. Then ask Him to help you, comfort you, heal you, and sustain you as you take the bold, beautiful risks that love requires. Lastly, ask Him to help you give yourself grace and space to feel the feelings that come along with those risks.

DAY 52

When you think about the life you want to live, and the woman you want to be, does the way you're living your life today match up with that? None of us are perfect (and we never will be!), but we usually have a good idea of when we're headed in the right direction and when we're just . . . not.

Have an honest conversation with God about it. Is there anything you're doing in your life that you know isn't good for you and doesn't line up with the woman you want to be? Share those things with God today, and then ask Him for the help you need to make the changes you know you want to make.

DAY 53

Take a few minutes to write yourself a note full of the encouragement you need to hear today. Then once you're finished, read it out loud to yourself. (Extra credit if you read it to yourself in the mirror!)

EVERY SINGLE MOMENT

180

DAY 54

There were a few times in my life when people I really loved and trusted told me that I was high maintenance. I don't know if those people even remember saying those words, if they meant them in the moment, or if they were ever true, but it didn't matter. Those words stuck with me for years and left me believing that I was too much work for anyone to truly love.

Friend, has this ever happened to you? When you think back, have there been words that people have said to you that have changed the way you see yourself? Tell God about anything that comes to mind and invite Him into it. Ask Him to heal those wounded places and to replace those ideas with His truth about who you really are.

DAY 55

Psalm 139:14 says that you are wonderfully made. What would it look like for you to take one step closer to believing that those words are true? And not about people in general, or about your girlfriends, or about your sister, but true about you. In the space below, write, "I am wonderfully made." You can write it once, or you can write it as many times as you need to, but let those words wash over you today.

EVERY SINGLE MOMENT

DAY 56

I have a bold dare for you. Ready? I dare you to write down three reasons why you are a total catch and an incredible person to be in a relationship with. You might feel shy about calling out your own great qualities, but you definitely have some and they're worth noticing and celebrating! After all, you're made in the image of God, and He says that His creation is good.

If your inner critic is particularly loud these days, it may take you a few minutes to think of three things. I've been there before, but stick it out. There are a million things you could write down today. Give yourself the time you need to think of three.

DAY 57

What's one thing you love about your appearance? Spend some time telling God about it today, and then thank Him for the way He made you. The way He made you isn't just good enough. It's spectacular.

_____

_____

_____

_____

_____

_____

_____

_____

_____

_____

_____

_____

_____

_____

_____

_____

_____

_____

_____

_____

DAY 58

Over the last week, you've written lots of encouraging words to yourself. But today, go one step deeper. Use your words to pour love into the areas of your heart where you need it the most by writing a love letter to yourself. This may feel a little bit awkward, or a tad uncomfortable, but this exercise made an enormous difference in the way I see and treat myself, and I'm praying it does the very same thing for you.

A Season of Dating

Dear Friend,

I always say that the process of meeting your future husband is one part God, one part you. It's one part God because, let's face it, for two compatible people to be at the right place, at the right time, and in the right season of life to meet each other is a total miracle. These are stories only God could weave together.

But you have a crucial part to play too. The only way you're going to be in that right place at that right time as the right person for your person is if you are living and growing into the woman God created you to be—trying things, taking risks, and meeting new people.

Now, can I be honest here? There were seasons of my life when I did not do this well.

There were seasons when I was putting myself out there maybe a little too much, times when my motivation was all wrong. Sometimes I was dating someone new because I was desperately trying to forget about someone old. (It never worked.)

Other times I sought out relationships because I was feeling lonely or extra insecure. The attention made me feel better (at least temporarily).

I really needed to take a step back in those seasons. I needed some time and space for me and God to work out some things together. I needed to deal with my past, to make some changes in my present, and to really invest in myself before I could invite someone into my future.

But there were also times when I swung a little too far in the other direction and didn't date even though I was fully ready to.

I'd done the work, I'd grown in so many ways, I'd healed from so many things, I really was ready for a relationship. But I found myself making all kinds of excuses for why I should wait just a little bit longer: maybe after I move, or start this new job, or maybe after the holidays. My reasons went on and on. But the real reason I put off dating was that I was afraid of being rejected. If I wasn't trying, I couldn't fail, right? Ever use that logic?

I was so afraid of rejection that I stopped participating in my love story altogether. I didn't want to put myself out there, I wanted someone to come to me with a risk-free guarantee. I was really hoping that God would plop the perfect guy right there on the doorstep of my comfort zone when the time was right.

The only problem is, that's not how God typically works. God invites us into the process. We have a part to play. He doesn't want us to be puppets in our love stories, He wants us to participate. And I'm so glad He does because through the participation comes preparation. God prepares us for what's next on the journey, and if we skip ahead toward the person we're going to marry, we won't be ready once we meet him.

I slowly began putting myself out there after I had this realization. When I started participating in my love story again, beautiful things began to happen.

Over the next several days, we are going to dive into your feelings about dating, your fears of rejection, your past hurts, and your future hopes. My prayer is that you be totally honest with yourself and with God, and that you walk out of this section with peace, clarity, and excitement for the next chapter of your love life.

Love,

Stephanie

DAY 59

How is your love life these days? Are you interested in someone? If so, who? Maybe you are feeling deeply single and you're so frustrated by this whole thing that you want to swear off dating for good? Tell God what's going on in your love life these days.

_____

_____

_____

_____

_____

_____

_____

_____

_____

_____

_____

_____

_____

_____

_____

_____

_____

_____

DAY 60

Isaiah 61:1, a prophecy about Jesus' coming, says, "The Spirit of the Sovereign Lord is on me, because the Lord has anointed me to proclaim good news to the poor. He has sent me to bind up the brokenhearted, to proclaim freedom for the captives and release from darkness for the prisoners" (NIV). Jesus came to do those things for you, all you have to do is ask Him.

Are there any broken places in your heart that you need God to heal? Are there any past experiences from your dating life or from your life in general that you know you need to sort through before you'll be able to be in a healthy relationship? Are there any areas of your life where you need to be set free? Spend some time asking today.

DAY 61

One of my all-time favorite verses is Romans 8:28. It's the verse I stand on when I have no idea where I'm going or what God might be up to. It's also the verse I grip onto the tightest when life feels scary, sad, or totally overwhelming. It says, "And we know that in all things God works for the good of those who love him, who have been called according to His purpose" (NIV). When is a time you've seen God make something beautiful out of something broken? Take a moment to remember today.

DAY 62

Are there any past mistakes you've made that you can't stop thinking about? Tell God about them, and then ask Him for forgiveness. Ask Him to help you use that situation to grow. Then, let yourself off the hook. God has forgiven you. It's time for you to forgive yourself too.

DAY 63

Spend a few minutes reflecting on how you've been showing up for your life. Have you been an active participant in your love life? Have you been intentionally working towards the future you're hoping for? Or are you hanging back, hoping God plops the right guy on your front doorstep? (Like I did for so long!)

Write two or three things that have been holding you back, and then ask God to help you break through those barriers so you can begin taking the big steps that only you can take toward the life and the relationship of your dreams.

DAY 64

You've prayed and asked God to help you boldly step forward into the life He's created you to live. So, how do you think dating fits into that? Do you think you're ready to date and be in a relationship?

It's easy to think there's a "right" answer here, or a perfect time to start dating, but what if God was more concerned with your heart and your motivations instead of whether you've completed a list of prerequisites?

Take some time to journal through the questions below and ask God for wisdom on how to move forward.

If you are dating right now, why are you dating? What is your motivation? On the flip side, if you aren't dating, why aren't you dating? What's your motivation there? Are you taking some intentional time to heal and grow in ways you know are really important? Or are you making excuses because you're afraid?

DAY 65

When you think about the prospect of meeting someone new, going on a first date, and maybe even starting a relationship, does any part of it scare you? Tell God about any fears that come to mind and ask Him for help with them.

DAY 66

The most frustrating thing about dating is that even when you finally muster up the courage to put yourself out there, there are still so many ways it can go awry. You're looking for the person who's your person, and along the way, you find all kinds of people who aren't. After a string of awkward first dates, ghosted text threads, or unrequited crushes (the worst!), discouragement tends to seep in. Spend some time talking with God about any discouragement you may be feeling right now, and then ask Him to re-fill you with the hope and energy you need to keep courageously putting yourself out there. Both the journey and the destination will be worth the perseverance they require.

DAY 67

The fear of rejection holds so many great people back, especially in dating. It makes sense, doesn't it? Rejection is painful. None of us want to experience it! But the worst part is the thoughts that follow in rejection's wake. We start thinking things like, "Of course they don't want me! Who would? Nobody wants me! I'm unlovable." But my friend, listen to me: this is not the truth. Rejection does not equal being unlovable! It just means it wasn't the right fit. You are a wonderful person, a total catch. You have so much to offer a relationship (and the world!). To the right person, you will be the right person. Take a few minutes to reflect on this with God today.

DAY 68

What's something good that's happening in your life these days? It can be something about your love life or something totally different! Tell God about your joy and take a moment to really celebrate it!

DAY 69

When all of your girlfriends, siblings, and Facebook friends seem to be getting married at the same time, it's easy to feel like you're falling behind in life (which of course puts a ton of pressure on every date and takes all the fun out of it). But Friend, I promise you're not. You're not falling behind, you're not falling short, and you haven't missed your chance. God is writing a beautiful story in your life, and the timing will be perfect.

Proverbs 3:5 says, "Trust in the Lord with all your heart," (NIV) but that's easier said than done—especially when you're trying to muster up the faith and patience on your own! Take a few minutes to pray for His perfect help as you learn to trust God's perfect timing.

_____

_____

_____

_____

_____

_____

_____

_____

_____

_____

DAY 70

In God's economy, there's more than enough to go around. That means that, as a believer, you get to feel joy when you see God do something amazing in someone else's life. That's a pretty amazing gift, isn't it? This is evidence of how big and powerful and amazing and loving our God is.

And here's the great news: God doesn't pick favorites—He is faithful to all of His children. Take a few minutes to reflect on this with God today.

DAY 71

One of the best ways to trust in God's faithfulness is to remember all the times He has been faithful in the past. Make a list of a few of the times that God has been faithful in your life, and come back to this list whenever you need a reminder of the fact that God is so, so good.

DAY 72

One of the hardest parts about singleness is the loneliness that often comes with it. It's not there all the time, but sometimes late at night or at a family wedding or when you are surrounded by happy couples, the loneliness can feel palpable. Take a few minutes today to tell God how you're doing with loneliness, and then ask Him for the comfort you need.

DAY 73

You know what everyone needs to hear sometimes? That they matter. You matter. You really do. You are special, wonderful, beautiful, and you make a difference. You are seen, known, loved, and the world is a better place because you're here. Spend a few moments reflecting on those truths with God today.

EVERY SINGLE MOMENT

DAY 74

James 1:5 says, "If any of you lacks wisdom, you should ask God, who gives generously to all without finding fault, and it will be given to you" (NIV). Are there any areas of your life (or your love life) where you need some wisdom right now? Take a few minutes to ask for it today.

DAY 75

Meeting guys is hard, right? Most women have no clue (not one!) where to meet an awesome guy. It just feels so daunting. But the beautiful thing is that you're not in this alone. Pray a bold prayer today and ask God for more opportunities to meet great men. And then (this part is super important), ask God for the courage to run with the opportunities you're given.

DAY 76

The idea of opening yourself up to someone is so darn scary, especially if you've been hurt in the past. While it is truly terrifying at times, it's also crucially important because real, true love can't exist without vulnerability. The journey of love can be painful and risky, but the destination is absolutely worth it. Pray that God would help you be brave and bold, and that He would help you continue being vulnerable and taking the risk.

DAY 77

Think about a time in the past when things didn't happen how you wanted them to, but in hindsight, you can see that it's way better this way. Pray and thank God for having better plans for your life than you could ever dream up on your own.

Looking Toward Marriage

Dear Friend,

I have a feeling you're going to love this next section. Over the past several weeks, you've done such hard work praying through your past and savoring your present. Today, it's time to start praying for your future and for the amazing man you'll share it with!

I'm praying that this is such a fun section for you—that you're able to connect with God in a deeper, more intimate way as you dream together about what the future could hold. I'm praying that this section brings you closer to God and fills you with hope for your future.

As you're praying for your future, you're going to be identifying some specific traits you're looking for in a future husband. This is super important because when you don't know what you're looking for, it's really hard to know when you've found it. And as we'll talk about in just a few days, it's really hard to settle for the wrong guy when you're praying for the right one.

These prayers will form a filter for you, helping you date with more clarity and direction. They'll help you really identify what you're looking for, so you can start praying for it; partnering with God as you keep an intentional eye out for the person who might end up being yours.

As I was writing the prayer prompts for this section, I went back and looked in my own journal for the prayers I prayed for my husband before I met him.

I found this one prayer in particular that made me laugh and cry in the exact same moment because those words—words I prayed months before meeting my husband—describe him perfectly.

What stuck out to me like crazy is the realization that I knew what I was looking for by then. I chose the words in that prayer so carefully. The attributes I asked God to grow in my future husband weren't random—they were hard-won bits of wisdom compiled over years of failed relationships, starts and stops, and broken hearts. I got to learn what was the most important to me, and then I prayed for exactly that.

I love that I took the time to think through this, that I carved out the space to really learn from my past relationships. And I love that these are the things I was so intentionally praying for in my future husband.

I love them because this is exactly who my husband is. God answered this prayer so clearly and directly, personally and beautifully.

I fully believe He'll do the same for you.

So, are you ready? Let's dive in.

Love,

Stephanie

DAY 78

What are some things you're looking forward to about being married? How do you hope the relationship will feel? What experiences or passions do you hope to share with your person? Spend a few minutes dreaming with God about those things today. Remember, relationships and marriage are good things. It's more than okay to want them!

DAY 79

What are some qualities that you are really hoping to find in your future husband? Kindness, strength, courage, integrity? A sense of humor, a love for adventure, a passion for family? Spend some time making a list with God, and then pray that He'll help you meet someone with those qualities.

DAY 80

You've made a list of traits you want in a future husband. You want someone who's kind, loving, and honest (and more!), and those are great things! Marriage is a big decision, and it's important to know what you're looking for.

The trouble comes when that perfectly fine, must-have list get a bit too long and a bit too specific.

There was a time when I thought I could not possibly marry someone who wasn't 6'2", blond, and a youth pastor. But if I had kept my list this specific, I would have missed out on meeting my amazing husband, Carl—a man who is not blond or a youth pastor, but who is absolutely perfect for me.

Pray that you wouldn't settle for any less than you deserve, but also that you'd have an open mind and heart so that God can surprise you with someone who's better than you ever could have dreamed up on your own.

DAY 81

What are some things you want to be true about your future marriage? If you aren't sure where to start, try thinking about it this way: When people interact with you and your husband, what do you want them to say about the way you love each other? Take some time to make a list and then pray for those things today.

_____

_____

_____

_____

_____

_____

_____

_____

_____

_____

_____

_____

_____

_____

_____

_____

_____

_____

DAY 82

I had a friend once say, "The longer you wait to meet your future husband, the longer you have to pray . . . for your future mother-in-law." Wise advice, my friend. Wise advice. They say that when you marry a person, you're also marrying their family, and it's so true. Take some time today to pray for your future in-laws and for the relationship you'll have with them someday. Then, spend a few minutes praying for the relationship your future husband will have with your family too!

DAY 83

Is there anything you've seen in someone else's relationship or marriage that you hope to emulate in your own someday? Is there anything you've seen that you don't want to emulate? Make a list of whatever comes to mind, and then ask God for help with both.

DAY 84

Are you hoping to have kids someday? If so, what kind of dad do you hope your future husband will be? Spend some time praying about that today. Pray for the man your future husband is today, and that God would help him become the man and the father your future children need him to be.

DAY 85

Spend a few minutes praying for your future family as a whole—for your future husband and for your future kids (if you decide to have them!). Pray for the kind of family you hope to be, the ways you hope to treat one another, and for the legacy you hope to create.

DAY 86

Is there any part of you that's afraid to get married? Is there anything about marriage that scares you? If so, know that you are so not alone. Invite God into those scared, anxious places. Talk to Him about any fears you may have and ask Him to fill those anxious places with peace. (Oh, and when you're finished, go check out Isaiah 43:2.)

DAY 87

Life is so much better when we have people in our corner, and this is especially true when it comes to marriage. When you think about your future marriage, what kind of support system do you hope the two of you have? What do you hope your friendships look like as a couple? Take some time to pray for that community today. Ask God to surround you with wonderful people who you can invest in and who will also invest in you.

DAY 88

Do you have a couple to mentor you when it comes to relationships? Trust me, they are worth their weight in gold when you can find the right fit. A couple who sets a great example of marriage will be invaluable for you both in the early stages of a committed relationship and long past your wedding day! If you don't have these mentors, spend a few minutes asking God to bring an older, wiser couple into your life.

DAY 89

Take the next few minutes to pray for your future husband—wherever he might be. Pray for his heart, for his faith, for the things that might be happening in his life right now, and whatever else comes to mind! Pray that he's using this season before he meets you to grow, to heal, and to become the very best version of himself, knowing that his life today and your future marriage will be so much better as a result.

A Life of Celebration

Dear Friend,

You've reached the end. Can you believe it? I'm so proud of all the hard work you've done over the last few months! I hope you're proud of yourself too.

Things have changed in your heart since you started here. You have changed. You've prayed some bold prayers, faced some hard things, and invited God into them. You've started embracing yourself, your God, and your life today in a whole new way. I love that.

All too often, people talk about singleness like it's a waiting room, but you've taken big, decisive steps into the truth that it's supposed to be so much more than that.

You've decided that this season while you're single is a time of preparation. It's a time of learning, of growing, and of becoming.

You know that who you become while you're single is who you will be when you're married, so you've decided to invest in your life in ways that will have a significant impact on your future marriage and your future family as well.

Friend, as you're finishing up this journal, I want to give you a wide-open space to celebrate all that you've walked through over the last few months. I want to give you the space to process what you've learned, how you've changed, and how you've grown.

The things you've learned in this season of journaling are going to impact the rest of your life—far beyond when you get married. The truth is that no matter if you're single, dating, engaged, or married, there's always an unknown season just around the corner, and you will always need faith, hope, and wisdom to guide you through.

As I was thinking about that the other day, I wondered what I would tell my future self if I could? In pretty much every season of life, I've needed the same reminder: to take a deep breath, to relax, and to make the most of the season I've been given. I would remind myself that I can trust God with both my present and my future, that every single time I have trusted Him with a piece of my life, what He's had for me was beyond anything I ever could have asked for or imagined. This time will be too.

I always need this reminder. Maybe you do too.

So, Friend, take this time to celebrate and remember, to look back and look ahead.

Today, pray that God would help you as you finish this prayer journey and launch into what's next. Ask Him to help you be brave and bold and intentional with this next chapter. Ask Him to help you do the things you know you need to do to become the woman you want to be.

Know that I'm praying alongside you every step of the way.

All my love,

Stephanie

DAY 90

Spend a moment looking back on your prayers from the first few days of this journey. How were you feeling when you started this prayer journal? What were you wrestling with back then? Now, take some time to reflect with God on all that's changed in these last few months. What have you seen change in your life as you've been on this journey with Him?

DAY 91

You have prayed a lot of prayers over the last few months (90 to be exact!). What prayers have you seen God answer along the way? Take some time to look back and to thank God today.

DAY 92

What's one way you've grown over the last three months? What's something you've learned or accomplished? What's something you've done that you're really proud of? Growth like this is hard-won and precious. Take some time to celebrate with God today.

DAY 93

What's one thing you've really loved about the last three months of your life?

_____

_____

_____

_____

_____

_____

_____

_____

_____

_____

_____

_____

_____

_____

_____

_____

_____

DATE:

DAY 94

How has your relationship with God changed over the last few
months? What have you seen transform and unfold in your heart
as you've been spending more time with Him? Thank God for what
He's done, and then pray a bold prayer and ask Him to take you
even deeper!

DAY 95

What's a lesson you've learned over the last three months that you want to make sure you never forget? Write it in the space below! Then, tell God about that lesson today and ask Him to cement it into your heart and your mind.

DAY 96

When you meet your husband someday, and you're looking back on this season of your life, what do you hope to be able to tell him about it?

DAY 97

After going through this prayer journey for the last few months, if you got a text from a friend who was feeling totally frustrated with her single life, what encouragement would you give her?

DAY 98

On every journey there are days when you feel strong and confident, like you could take on the world. There are also days when you feel frustrated, lost, and ready to give up, like you've lost all the ground you just gained.

If you find yourself feeling this way, know that you're not alone, you're not doing things wrong, and you haven't lost all the progress you've made along the way. This is a normal part of the journey. Some days are just harder than others.

But with that in mind, take a few minutes today to write yourself a pep talk that you can read on those discouraging days.

DAY 99

When you look toward the future, what do you hope your life looks like one year from today? What do you want to have accomplished? What kind of community do you hope surrounds you? Where do you want to be in your career, in your relationship with God, in your relationship with yourself? Take some time to dream with God, and then, write down one small step you can take today that will start you on your way.

DAY 100

Last, but certainly not least, I invite you to write yourself one final love letter. Spend a few minutes reminding yourself what you've learned and walked through over the last few months, how you've changed, grown, and some tools you can take with you along the way. Remind yourself of how much God loves you and how much you love you! Remind yourself of all the reasons you have to be excited, joyful, and hopeful in every single moment of your life.

Stephanie May Wilson is the go-to guide for 20 and 30-something women as they navigate their most important relationships. Through her book, The Lipstick Gospel, and her chart-topping podcast, Girls Night with Stephanie May Wilson, Stephanie has mentored thousands of women as they cultivate healthy, thriving relationships with God, friends, significant others, and themselves.

When she's not writing, speaking, or recording a podcast episode, Stephanie is usually packing for a global adventure with her husband Carl, laughing with her close tribe of girlfriends, or snuggled up in yoga pants in her Nashville home.